HURON COUNTY LIBRARY

S0-BYM-043

HURON COUNTY LIBRARY

2 008 061096 5

DISCARD

Date Due

HEN Oct 88		
FEB 3 1990		
JUN 09 199		
NOV 1 1 199		
DEC 2 3 1997		

BRODART, INC. Cat. No. 23 233 Printed in U.S.A

05605

917
.11
0440222
Hin

Hines, S.
British Columbia.

PRICE: $27.95   (06/he)

HEN Oct 88		
3536	FEB 3 1990	
JUN 09 199		
33899		

05605

917   Hines, Sherman, 1941-
.11   British Columbia / Sherman Hines ; foreword by
0440222 Jack Webster. -- Halifax, N.S. : Nimbus, c1988.
Hin   1 v. (unpaged) : all col. ill.

           "Previously published by McClelland and Stewart."
           03285596   ISBN:0920852815 (N)

           1. British Columbia - Description and travel - Views. I.
           Title

5434   88SEP02   06/he   1-00428552

DISCARD

British Columbia

British Columbia

Sherman Hines

Foreword by Jack Webster

05605

OCT 1 7 1988

NIMBUS PUBLISHING LIMITED

To my wife Andrea,
sons David and Andrew

Copyright © 1988 Sherman Hines

All rights reserved. The use of any part of this publication reproduced,
transmitted in any form or by any means, electronic, mechanical, photocopying,
recording, or otherwise, or stored in a retrieval system, without the prior
consent of the publisher is an infringement of the copyright law.

Nimbus Publishing Limited
P.O. Box 9301, Station A
Halifax, Nova Scotia
CANADA B3K 5N5

CANADIAN CATALOGUING IN PUBLICATION DATA

Hines, Sherman, 1941–
  British Columbia

ISBN 0-920852-81-5

1. British Columbia–Description and travel–
1981-   -Views.* I. Title.

FC3812.H56 1988   917.11'044'0222   C88-098518-6
F1087.8.H56 1988

Previously published by McClelland and Stewart Limited under ISBN 0-7710-4157-8
Printed and bound in Hong Kong
Colour separation by Hong Kong Graphic Arts Service Centre
Printing and binding by Everbest Printing Company Limited

Page 2: Trees at Macmillan Park, near Port Alberni.
Right: The Black Tusk.

Foreword

I tell stories for a living, and purely by the chance of blind choice do I live in British Columbia. It's a beautiful place by any definition. Surely that's obvious. Our mountains make the Swiss Alps look shabby.

I don't like picture books. Years ago I forbade my family to take photos of scenery. If you can't remember what you've seen you are over the hill. It's people who matter, not pictures. Most of what I have seen of B.C. has been through the eyes of a reporter, covering death, disaster, criminal activities, and assorted gross injustices, and there's nothing beautiful about mayhem in its various forms. From time to time, however, I have lifted my eyes to glory in the beauties of the best part of the entire world in which we live.

The Websters didn't come to Canada to admire the scenery. We followed an old Scotch tradition of migrating to Canada for the usual reasons – more room to breathe, fewer people, less competition, a new start, to pick up the gold off the streets, and last, but not least, to get away from the drab climate of the west of Scotland.

But if the truth were told, we came because of the Hollywood image of North America. Actually, we came to Vancouver because it was the closest place to California we could come without a visa. But we knew, too, that a man called John had gone from Glasgow to Canada a few years ahead of us and become prime minister.

And so our Swiss family Webster came to a Vancouver November, leaden skies and sodden streets at a time when post-war Canada was not yet in the high gear of post-war prosperity.

Our first home was an experience in the pioneer life – wood furnaces, sawdust stoves, and ice boxes. It was weeks before we learned to stack wood, or to feed the furnace slightly less than enough to drive us out to sit on the doorstep in the pouring rain for temporary coolness.

My introduction to the wilderness and grandeur of British Columbia was to come early in my years. For instance, as a reporter on *The Vancouver Sun* I was assigned to cover one whirlwind tour of B.C. by the attorney general of the day. The culture shock was considerable. Here was I, a stripling reporter who thought he'd been around, in the company of one of the world's great drinkers.

We started from Vancouver by train, making overnight hiccough and whistle stop appearances, as the great man denounced the social evils that would be cured by his magnanimous government. Policemen met us at each stop with fresh supplies of social evil.

Eventually we reached the then small cow town of Williams Lake but time demanded that we fly back to the coast immediately. Four of us boarded a tiny Seabee pusher plane. We took off in a squall for Bella Coola. Within minutes the weather closed in, and the pilot, unable to turn back, was forced to drop below mountain-top level while we fearfully charted a way through the coastal range.

The flight took us down one valley, two hundred feet above ground, and seemed to run smack into the mountain at the end of the valley, before turning to find Dean Channel, the escape route to the sea. That two-hour flight planted in me an admiration for bush pilots but also a grateful thanks-be to God for the technical improvements that now make such flights unnecessary and non-suicidal.

The Websters became outdoor enthusiasts and camped in many corners of the province. By the glittering lakes of Kalamalka and Okanagan, in the gravel beds of the Cariboo, never omitting to pan for gold in the places where, even in the thirties, hardy unemployed men could avoid the work camps and welfare handouts.

One time we decided to explore Wells Gray Park to see Helmcken, the highest waterfall in North America. From Vancouver we set out via Kamloops and Barrière. At Clearwater, the man at the gas station said, "Careful on that road. It's a bit tricky." What an understatement! In those far-off days, the road into Wells Gray was primitive: room for one car only on the highway, treacherous single-lane bridges and a drop off at the side that was, I swear, two hundred feet straight down. When you met a car coming the other way, the only way to pass was to back up and let the other guy crawl past on the outside of the narrow road.

It was simple to pitch our tent. We were the only humans, but not the only inhabitants, at the campsite at the Falls. The three small Webster children were happy. So were the bears. We had invited every black bear in Wells Gray for supper. They came in sizes large and small, timid and aggressive, with and without cubs, advancing and probing with the tenacity of an armoured division.

Your hero, guardian of the family whose sole defence was a hatchet, prepared to repel all bear boarders. It was not long before common sense took precedence over pride. The tent was unceremoniously struck, and I fled with the family into the night and the treacherous road back.

Year after year the Websters headed out into the interior of B.C., glorying in the lakes and the mountain tops. We learned to ride cowboy style round the barrels on the slopes above Quilchena. The cowboy life is great, if you don't have to do it for a living and can just pretend you're going to ride the fifty miles of range on which the five thousand or so head of cattle thrive.

Sometimes we saw British Columbia from the sea. There once was a wonderful old ship that somehow was brought here from the Great Lakes. She was the *Tahsis Prince*, a coastal freighter that sailed from Vancouver once a week to Bamfield, Ucluelet, Ahousat, Gold River, Nootka, and way points to Zeballos.

She carried food, booze, policemen, dentists, and other essentials. The galley was a community kitchen to use as you wished, helping yourself to the ship's stores. The crew were all descendants of the ancient mariner. They could splice anything from a mainbrace to a hawser.

One of the sights I'll never forget was at dawn on the channel sliding through the waters of Muchalat Inlet between Gold River and Tahsis and watching the antics of killer whales. Blackie the bo's'n said to me once, "The killer whales always show for us. They've seen us bouncing up and down on the west coast so often they think we're a killer whale, too!"

The *Tahsis Prince* was eventually wrecked near Ahousat.

She was written off as a dead loss, but was rescued by West Coast Indians and one day came chugging into North Vancouver for repairs and a large amount of salvage money. Though the crew used to talk of her as a coffin ship for fourteen men, never actually did she sink.

Once I naïvely accepted an invitation to be a crewman on a halibut boat for a week. Halibut, when catches are big, is the pure gold of the sea. Two-hundred-pound fish at two dollars a pound or more.

When I arrived in the northern port, and went to the local for a drink, I announced proudly my chosen vessel and other skippers looked at me askance and muttered: "Not that one, surely! Is your insurance up to date?"

Always a willing worker I instantly cleaned out the rotting rain gear and rubber boots of long dead men from the crew's quarters and I opened the skylight. That was a mistake. The dirt and grime of years had sealed it before and now it dripped sea water endlessly.

The first day out in the North Pacific was euphoric. The long slow swells were matched by the rhythmic surfacing of the purple dolphins sliding alongside the fishing boat like an escort of fighter planes. The second day was different and difficult. It blew seventy miles an hour. I swear I could see the wind as it pushed large jagged waves from the direction of the horizon straight at our pathetic seventy-foot antique fishing boat, smashing the protective sheathing at the stern of the boat, blowing the deck lifeboat into the sea, and causing panic in my landlubber's breast.

The captain jettisoned the twenty miles of hook and lines behind us, and jogged the old wooden ship into the wind. We were driven miles out into the Pacific. Seamanship and the laws of nature saw us through. The experience gave me a new respect for all fishermen. The radar was gone and the Loran was out of order. It would have been instant drowning had the ship gone over, as I knew it must. That night my fear was such that the skipper handed me a bottle of Chivas Regal. No one else touched it. I didn't get drunk. It did, however, prevent me from jumping over the side in panic.

But let's face it. I am basically a city slicker, more at home with people than panoramas. Once you've seen one mountain you've seen them all.

The cities and towns of B.C. are something else again. Never forget that Vancouver was founded by a gabby old bootlegger named Gassy Jack Deighton who trundled a barrel of whisky through the primeval forest from New Westminster to Vancouver in 1886. And when I came along in 1947, things hadn't changed all that much. There was a bootlegger in every alley, and a bookmaker in every corner smokeshop. Houses of ill repute were known to exist and prosper in the most unlikely areas, and illegalities were more controlled than suppressed. As a matter of fact, if you look down instead of up in certain parts of Vancouver you'll see the names of the madames still inscribed in tile on the doorsteps of certain homes.

My first major assignment as a reporter was to seek out the lawbreakers. It was too easy. Vancouver's finest stood guard on the biggest illegal bookie shop in town, which was jammed with betters listening to the off-the-track commentary from Santa Anita and queuing up at the two-dollar, five-dollar, and ten-dollar windows. Gambling clubs ran openly twenty-four hours round the clock. So-called private clubs served liquor to all comers.

I went back to my managing editor, the legendary Hal Straight, and complained, "No story. It can't be illegal. It's done in the open." He convinced me otherwise.

And the city was full of retired warriors of the rum-running days. Many of the big mansions were founded on the Volstead act, which brought prohibition to the United States. There is no prize for the person who finds the building in downtown Vancouver still faintly inscribed as the Kennedy Building (reputedly owned by John F's father to store scotch in Vancouver for the trade in high-speed launches down the coast).

And there were other more legitimate retired warriors from the Mackenzie-Papineau Battalion of Canadians who fought for the Republic in the Spanish Civil War. Before that they had taken part in the desperate trek on Ottawa in 1935 during an era in Vancouver now forgotten. They were decent unemployed workers who had occupied Vancouver's hotels and art galleries and the post office in peaceful protest until they were driven out by baton-wielding policemen.

But the face of Vancouver has changed for the better, too. Where once was drab row housing there now are the high rises.

But one change that should never have happened was to allow the moneyed hordes from the east to take downtown Vancouver and bury it (as they've done) in underground shopping malls. Our shoppers don't need that kind of protection from wintry blasts or suffocating heat.

Despite that aberration, Vancouver is shaping up. No other downtown in North America has such sparkling water on three sides.

But we still have swashbuckling politicians and labour leaders who buckle swashes. It's the climate, we think, that produces elected representatives who tend to gravitate to the outer edges on any spectrum. Some can even straddle the fence and have both feet on the ground at the same time.

Like the cabinet minister who said to me: "Webster, if I tell a lie it is only because I am sincerely convinced I'm telling the truth."

British Columbia is different.

Jack Webster

Overleaf: In late fall near Golden, only a few aspen still hold their leaves.

Left: Spring near Alliford Bay on the Queen Charlotte Islands.

Above: A cow moose in the early-morning light near Revelstoke.

Parliament buildings reflected in Victoria Harbour.

Sproatt Mountain after being windswept by a storm of driving snow.

Above: Storm clouds over the Cariboo Mountains, near Valemount.

Right: Moose Lake, Mount Robson Park.

Above: Moss-covered tree trunk in Stanley Park, Vancouver.

Right: Near Sitkum Creek along Highway 3A.

Cutting the corn crop for winter feed near Chilliwack.

The moon is already visible at sunset near Long Beach.

Left: Sunset at False Creek.

Above: Barnacles and mussels cling to the rocks near Ucluelet.

Left: Cormorants rest on a log near Queen Charlotte,
as the sun breaks through a cloud and hits the water.

Above: Sunset near Chilliwack.

Overleaf: Summit of Sproatt Mountain.

Sea lions leaping off rocks near Ucluelet.

Sea lions on Sea Lion Rock near Ucluelet, off the coast of Vancouver Island.

Above: A hoary marmot pauses for a brief moment
during the excavation of a new retreat.

Right: Moss and leaves covering the saw cuts on a tree stump.

Left: Ducks at sunrise, Prince Rupert.

Above: Atlin Lake.

Overleaf: Cargo ships and pleasure craft in English Bay.

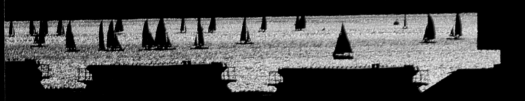

Leaves catch the water from a recent rain.

Spring and nature's own compost of dead leaves, moss and fungus.

Crops reflected in a pond in the Fort Nelson area.

Crops awaiting harvest near Fort Nelson.

Left: Moss-covered rocks near Revelstoke.

Above: Rainstorm near Hope.

Overleaf: CN Imax Theatre and the Vancouver skyline
from Stanley Park.

Left: Spring blossoms in the Butchart Gardens, Vancouver Island.

Above: Blackberries after the rain near Parksville, Vancouver Island.

Starfish and sea anemone on Sea Lion Rock, near Ucluelet.

Barnacles growing on the rocks near Tofino.

Above: Trees and rolling hills near Kamloops.

Right: Dutch Creek hoodoos and the Dutch Creek.

Sunlight reflected off the rocks beside Shannon Falls.

A moss-covered rock in a small brook in the rain forest
south of Prince Rupert along the inland waterway.

Above: Farmer harvesting crops near Fort Nelson.

Left: Building a log cabin near Lillooet.

Above: Small bushes reflect in the water of a brook
        near the Paint Pots in Kootenay National Park.

Right: Blue heron fishing for lunch near Tofino.

Canoe Mountain, near Valemount.

Above: Reflections in a brook near Whistler.

Overleaf: Moss growing on rocks near Revelstoke.

Left: Heli-skiing in the Cariboo Mountains, near Valemount.

Above: Tree shadows on the snow.

Above: Snow covers the rocks in a brook, Kootenay National Park.

Right: Frost crystals on the ice in a brook, Kootenay National Park.

Grenville Channel, inland waterway near Hartley Bay.

A ray of sunlight illuminates a patch of water and a seagull, Qualicum Beach.

Left: Lighthouse Park in West Vancouver.

Above: A mallard drake rests at sunset, Beacon Hill Park in Victoria.

Driftwood on the beach near Tlell in the Queen Charlotte Islands.

Driftwood near Tlell on the coastline of the Queen Charlotte Islands.

Left: David Jackson, carver and painter of wood, West Vancouver.

Above: Canada goose, carved and painted by David Jackson of West Vancouver.

Left: Trees near Whistler.

Above: Elk, near the B.C./Alberta border.

Overleaf: Mount Carter, near Atlin on the B.C./Yukon border.

Sunset near Blackcomb Peak.

Right: Early morning dew on a leaf, Stanley Park.

Above: Moss-covered tree roots, Stanley Park, Vancouver.

Above: From the summit of Sproatt Mountain, looking southwest.

Overleaf: Sunset on Sproatt Mountain.

Rocks beside a brook near Manning Park.

Dog team on the yearly mail run from Whitehorse to Atlin.

Left: Rainstorm in Yoho National Park.

Above: A totem pole in Stanley Park.

The Three Sisters Mountain, near Skidegate, Queen Charlotte Islands.

Fall colour at Moberly.

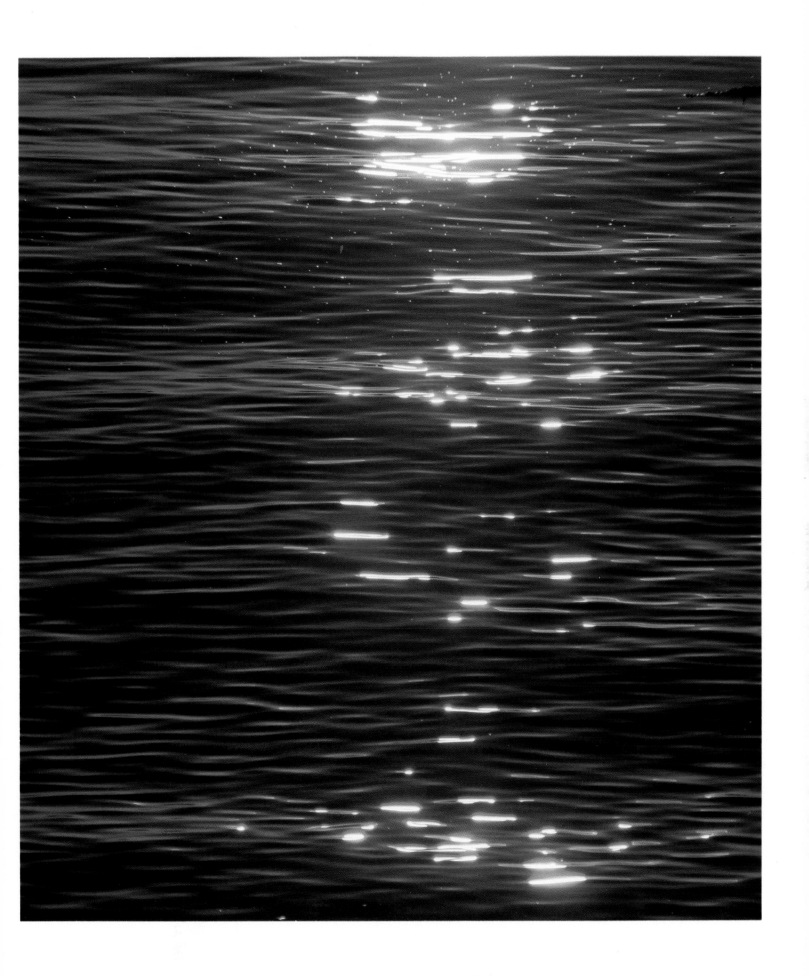

Above: Clouds over Christina Lake.

Left: The rays of the rising sun form a pattern on False Creek, Vancouver.

Above: Forest floor on Campania Island, south of Prince Rupert.

Right: The Paint Pots in Kootenay National Park were created by spring water
coming in contact with rich underground iron-ore deposits.

Sitkum Creek on Highway 3A.

Left: Moss on a Douglas fir and stump, Stanley Park.

Above: Skunk cabbage, one of the first signs of spring.

Overleaf: Frost-covered bush near Whistler.

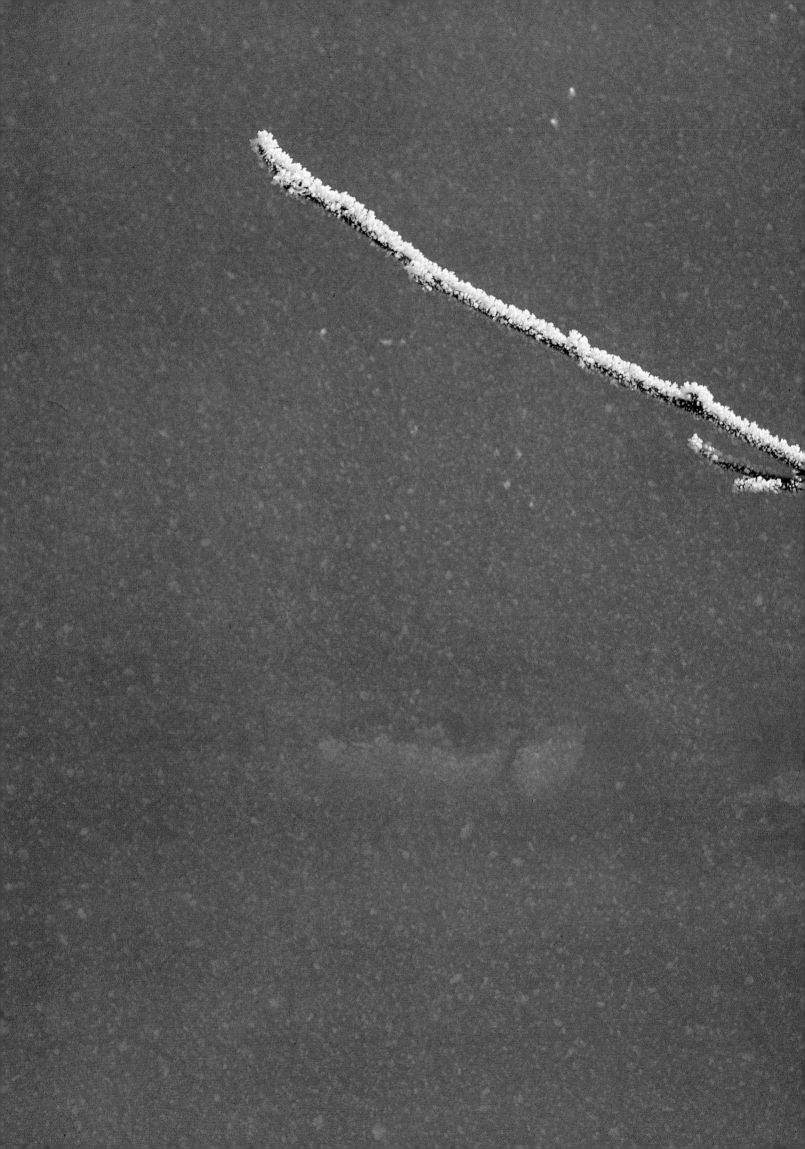

Left: The Black Tusk, near Whistler.

Above: The base of Shannon Falls.

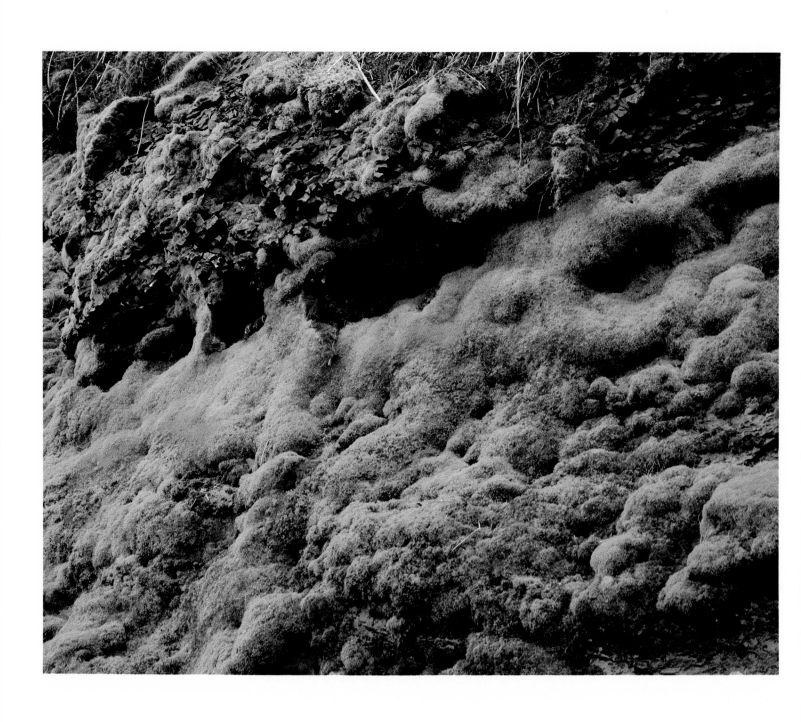

Spring water flows over moss-covered rocks, near Sandspit, Queen Charlotte Islands.

Horses graze peacefully on a farm near Moberly.

Left: Bridal Veil Falls.

Above: Water drops on trees near Wycliffe.

Above: Water striders skitter across the surface of a brook near Maureen Bridge.

Right: Spring near Alliford Bay on Moresby Island, Queen Charlotte Islands.

Sunflower crop near Keremeos.

Grapes bask in the sunlight in a vineyard near Kelowna.

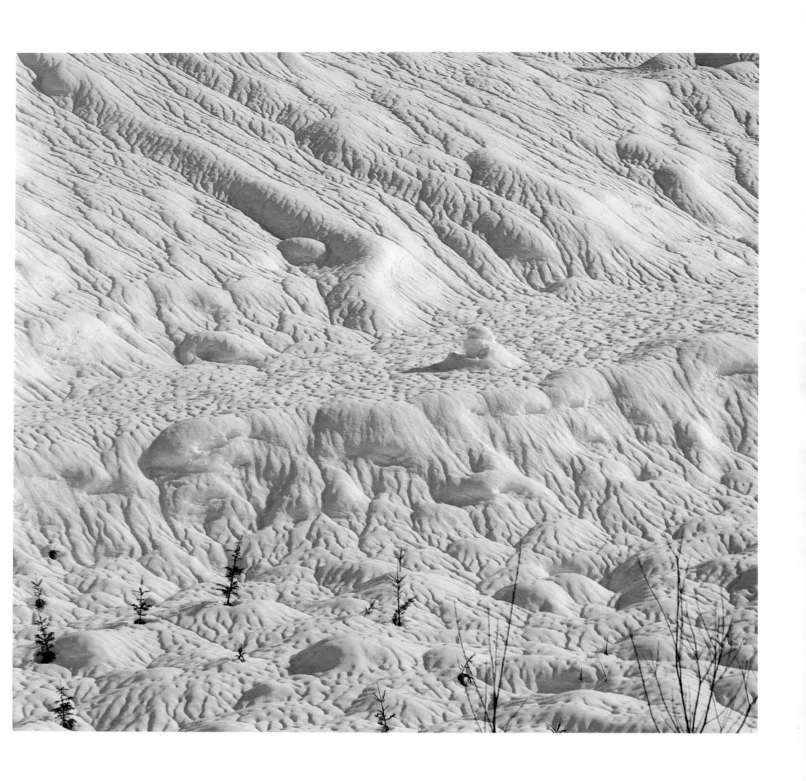

Left: Looking west from Blackcomb Peak.

Above: Snow in Garibaldi Park.

Left: Giant Douglas fir near Whistler.

Above: A raft of logs and reflections of clouds in Kootenay Lake.

Overleaf: Dawn near Golden.

An early-morning golfer in Stanley Park, Vancouver.

Cherry blossoms, a rain storm, and a brief moment of sunshine
at the Maritime Museum in Vanier Park, Vancouver.

Left: Blowing snow backlit by the sun near Field.

Above: Snow-covered trees on the summit of Sproatt Mountain.

Above: Sunset near Maureen Bridge on the road to the Pacific Rim National Park.

Right: Spring ice and foam in a brook near Revelstoke.

Rocky coastline of the Queen Charlotte Islands, near Sandspit.

Fireweed growing along a brook near Maureen Bridge, Vancouver Island.

Above: Morning sun through the mist near Delta.

Right: Rainstorm in Kootenay National Park.

Left: Logger on felled Sitka spruce, Gil Island.

Above: Cypress I in MacDonald Bay.

Twilight on a farm near Chilliwack.

Above: A field of hops near Chilliwack.

Overleaf: Early morning mist near Kamloops.

Above: Cargo ships await their turn to unload, English Bay.

Right: The water of Horseshoe Bay photographed through the leaves of a tree.

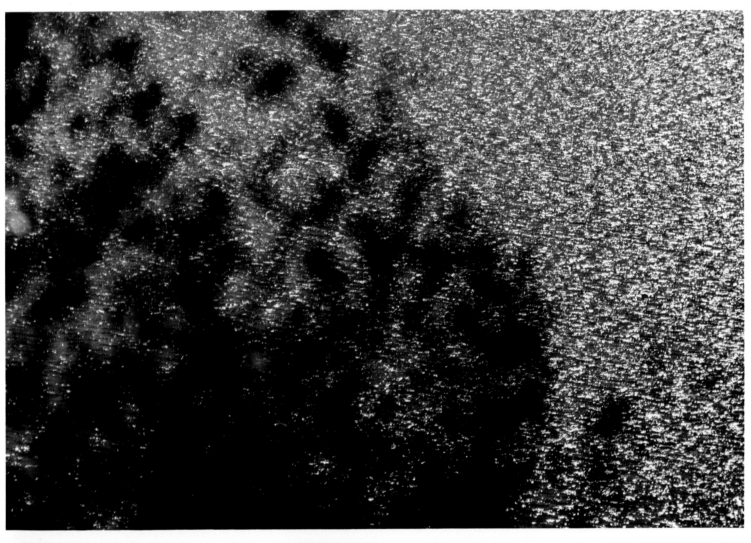
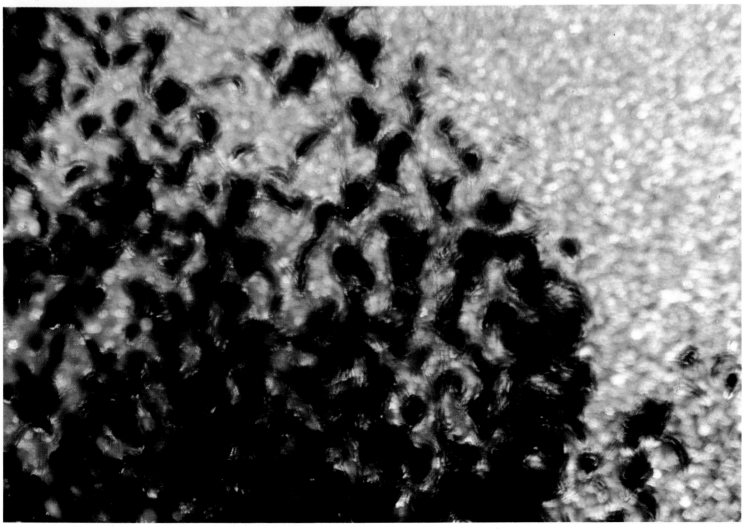

A brook along the highway to Squamish.

Fern glistens with water droplets from a recent rain.

Above: Forest on the highway between Whistler and Pemberton.

Right: Garibaldi Park.

Left: The setting sun highlights the sculptured snow on Mount Currie near Pemberton.

Above: Ranch buildings near Pemberton. Mount Currie is in the background.

Above: Sunset near Ucluelet, Vancouver Island.

Right: Fishing on Box Lake.

Light breaking through an opening in the clouds near English Bay.

Storm clouds over the Gulf Islands.

Left: Snow-covered tree near Atlin.

Above: Looking southwest from Sproatt Mountain, near Whistler.

Overleaf: Seagulls on log boom on Kootenay Lake.

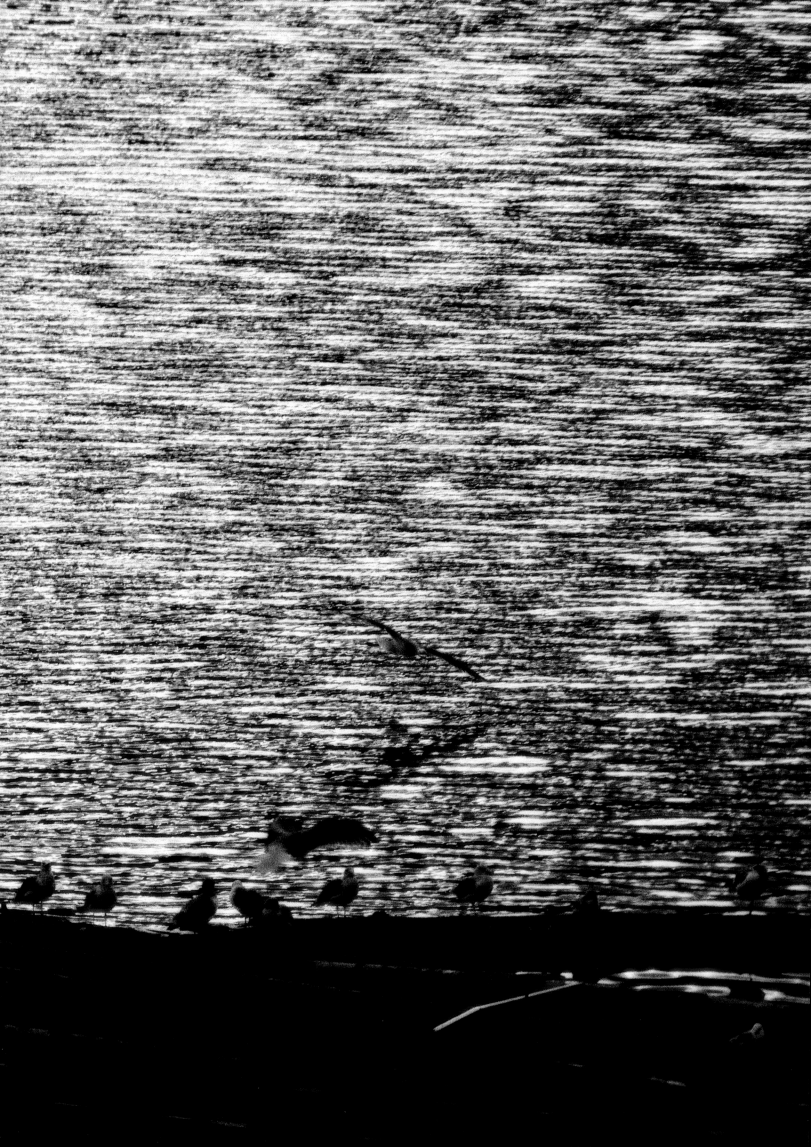

Left: Cariboo Mountains during a snowstorm.

Above: Spring break-up in a stream near Blackcomb Peak.

Atlin Lake and Mount Minto.

Straws in snow near Atlin.

Moose Lake in Mount Robson Park.

Sunset at Long Beach, Pacific Rim National Park on Vancouver Island.